Dancing in the Santa Ana Winds

Poems y Cuentos New and Selected

Also by liz gonzález

Beneath Bone

October 13, 2018

Dancing in the Santa Ana Winds

Poems y Cuentos New and Selected

Risa, I'm grateful to be working with you! May your words joyfully dance on the page fa years to come! Abrazos,

liz gonzález

liz gonzáz

Los Nietos Press
Downey California
2018

Published in the United States by
Los Nietos Press
Downey, CA 90240
www.LosNietosPress.com
LosNietosPress@gmail.com

Cover Photo - Front: liz gonzález
Cover Photo – Back and Spine: Jorge Martin

First Edition
ISBN-13: 978-0-9984036-4-9

for Mama, Dorothy Avance
Hija de Serrano

Contents

Contents (Cont.)

Dancing in the Santa Ana Winds

Dancing in the Santa Ana Winds

The same wind that uproots trees
makes the grasses shine.
—Rumi, "The Grasses"

Death and taxes. Some say that's all you can depend on in life. If you live in the Inland Empire or Los Angeles County, you can also count on the Santa Ana winds blowing every year, September through May. Those of us who grew up here don't underestimate the Santa Anas; we've witnessed their destructive power. But we natives don't lose our heads during these winds, either, as some authors have led outsiders to believe. We adjust.

On school mornings when the Santa Anas began to puff, Grandma would weave my little sister's and my waist-length hair into two braids, one sprouting from each side of our head. She would get my little sister and me ready for school because Mama had to leave early for work. Grandma pulled my hair back so tight that when she finished, I'd check my reflection in the bathroom mirror to see if my eyebrows had stretched into my temples. Our walk to and from Myers Elementary School was about twenty minutes each way. The Santa Anas pushed us hard, as though they might lift us into the sky and toss us around like paper kites. By the time I reached home at the end of the day, my braids had long been unraveled, and the tangled mess at the back of my head bulged out like a fallen beehive hairdo.

Those nights were miserable. After a full day at work, cooking dinner, and washing dishes, Mama would sit on the toilet seat to comb the "Charlies" out of my hair. She named the tangles at the back of my head after the mats Charlie, our long-haired collie, would get in his coat. I'd stand with my back to her and cry as she sprayed a detangling product into my hair and coaxed out the knots little by little. What seemed like an hour later, she could finally run the comb through my product-drenched hair.

Fed up with my Charlies, one Saturday morning Mama drove me to the beauty shop and told the hairdresser to cut my hair up to my neck, perhaps in a bob. The hairdresser recommended I also get a perm to thicken my fine, flat hair and make it harder to tangle. Although money was tight, Mama gave her the go ahead. The result: Imagine a black alpaca's head of hair stiffened with a coat of lacquer. I must not have minded too much. In all the photos of me taken that summer during a trip to Mexico with my grandparents, I'm wearing a big grin.

We lived on the Bench during those years, an area by the Lytle Creek Wash at the west end of San Bernardino and a few blocks from the Rialto border. Across the street from our house was a large vacant lot that stretched the length of our block. Eucalyptus trees lined the lot, a windbreak for the crops that had been cleared a decade or so earlier. A field of grasses replaced the crops. In the three-digit summer heat, the sun baked the grasses a golden yellow. At least once every fall, the field erupted in fire. It was expected, just part of the season, and the families who lived on our street didn't fear our homes would burn down. Soon the whine of the fire truck's siren would alert us that help was on the way. We neighborhood children and the grown-ups stepped out our front doors, stood on our front lawns, or walked over to a neighbor's lawn, and chatted as we watched the firemen put out the fire. For weeks after, the smell of wet burnt grass permeated the air, stayed stuck in our sinuses, and traveled with us in our dreams.

Mornings after the Santa Anas had been especially raucous, the front page of the local newspaper displayed photos of the damage. Large tree branches landed on front lawns or blocked streets. Sometimes a tree uprooted and crashed through the roof of a home, knocked over power lines, or squashed a car. Then there were the wildfires fanned by the Santa Anas. In the last hundred years or so, most fires have been caused by humans. Lives were lost and whole neighborhoods destroyed. My godparents' home was one of the few left standing in their area after the Panorama Fires in 1989. Are the Santa Anas to blame for the destruction caused by fires set by humans? Are we in the way of the Santa Anas and fires, or are they in our way? These questions are explored in many news outlets during major fires, only to be explored again when the next fire occurs.

Fortunately, most years the damage from the Santa Anas is minor. Some of us are physically more impacted than others though. They give me headaches. When the Santa Anas blow, I shut myself indoors, switch on the humidifier, open the curtains, and watch the show. The Santa Anas play magnificent music, too, using objects in their path as an instrument. I often join the revelry and dance—in my controlled indoor environment.

Most everything dances in the Santa Anas. Bunches of purple needlegrass glimmering on hillsides bend in a sideway mountain yoga pose. Dried sycamore leaves get dragged over sidewalks, their tips scratch the cement like claws. Palm tree fronds thrash like diehard headbangers. Freed tumbleweeds bounce across streets with reckless abandon. Bougainvillea petals and camellia blossoms fly off branches and scatter across the lawn, like confetti bursting from cracked cascarónes at an Easter celebration.

When the Santa Anas have mellowed, some of us head to one of the nearby hiking trails. At the top of a hill, we pause and inhale deep the clear view of the mountains, high rises, and Pacific Ocean: Southern California in all its glory.

Best Granddaughter

I

Years before surgeons
cut the lump
out of your trachea,
I promised vigilance
by your deathbed.

My devotion for you crying,
"Lichee, Lichee!" nights
after my father died when I was three,
for stepping into his place
the times Mama let you,
for giving me understanding
instead of scoldings.

I should have known
I would never come through.
Whenever Grandma took
afternoons off to shop
during my school breaks,
I dreaded the simple responsibility
of boiling two weenies
and water for a steaming coffee cup.
Your lunch stunk up the kitchen.

II

"Television wastes the mind," you used to say.
You wrote through mornings,
then stretched in a metal lawn chair
beneath bougainvillea-laced shadows

and read The Sun-Telegram, classic novels,
and the German version of LIFE
—your hearing aid humming.

You taught me how to type,
play dominoes and checkers,
and keep a personal budget—
even my one cent
bubble gum had to be recorded.
You assigned me to read the newspaper
and books in your glass door bookcase.
I foolishly turned down
your guitar and mandolin lessons.

III

After your surgery,
on one of my infrequent visits,
I brought my VCR,
The Sound of Music, and *The Red Shoes*—
the two films you deemed worthy
of taking us granddaughters
to the downtown theater to see.

Nino dressed you in layers of clothes,
wrapped you in a blanket
to keep you from shivering.
I hadn't considered
you were too weak to watch movies
and rose only for me.

I couldn't cross four feet of aqua carpet
to wipe the spittle dripping down your chin.
To make up for it,

I volunteered to squeeze
your two o'clock feeding.
Impatience wasn't the reason
I pushed the plastic scented liquid
that prolonged your dying
into your belly too quickly,
jutting your spine,
your gasp
toward the ceiling.

IV

Friday morning, April 13,
one of my sisters called to alert me:
Grandma decided
to admit you to a nursing home.
You agreed.
I knew you'd let go
before the white uniforms
pushed a gurney beside
your rented hospital bed.

You told me at 8:57 that night.
Whipped branches on my window.
9 exactly, the ring
smashed the darkness.
Mama on the other end:
"It's time."

The Santa Fe whistle blew
quitting hour
when my tires finally snapped
Grandma's driveway gravel
Saturday evening.

If I had left after Mama's call,
I would have arrived
before the coroner
and mortuary men.
I could have hugged you
goodbye.

"Now your grandpa
will never get to walk you
down the aisle."
Grandma's front door greeting.

V

Some family members contested
my qualifications to stand on the altar
at your funeral mass.
A Mary Magdalene tainting
the family name.
Upright at the jade marble lectern,
zipped into a tailored dress,
your requirement
for family occasions,
I sucked the incense deep,
told tales from the memoir
you typed on your Royal manual
about your childhood in the Midwest,
before San Bernardino
and Grandma.
Pages you shared with nobody,
except me.

Stepping off the train
at the Topeka depot in 1911
after a three-day trip
from San Francisco del Rincon
with your mother, little brothers,
sister, and cousin
to join your father—
a laborer for Santa Fe.
The moves to Missouri, Nebraska,
Iowa, and Minnesota—
wherever your father found work.
The biting cold boxcar homes.
The German Catholic school in Waterloo
and donated Thanksgiving turkey
that your mother
"cooked Mexican style with mole poblano."
Your summer jobs—
water-boy, lantern-boy, farm hand,
helping your dad in his barber shop/pool hall.
The day you had to return your books
to Omaha Technical High School
where you played clarinet
in the orchestra and band.
Your family needed your wages.

Everyone in the church listened
Even the children stayed hushed.
I glanced at your casket before me
and flashed back to when I'd spot you
in the audience at all my school presentations.
No smile on your face, but I knew
I made you proud, like I did today.

Buñuelos

Grandma stands at the kitchen counter
like a luchador in an apron, ready for a match.
She slaps stretched dough onto its back,
rolls a hacked-off broomstick end over the top,
twists to the stove, and slides
the full-moon tortilla into an iron pan.
Boiling oil swallows, spits, hisses
until the tortilla blisters, crisps.
She dips her pincher fingers in quick,
snatches the crunchy wafer from its bath,
flips it onto a paper towel lined plate,
slathers the top with cinnamon-piloncillo syrup,
and plops the sweet treat on the plastic
pink placemat in front of me. I blow on it,
pick it up with both hands, and take a bite.
The buñuelo breaks into a hundred pieces.
I lick up the crumbs, sugar, my sticky fingers.
Grandma leaps back to the counter
for another smackdown.

The Four Food Groups in Grandma's Summer Lunches

L-
ard
fried thick
slabs of Spam,
toast brown, or eggs
scrambled with tuna or
canned green beans, or both.
Wash it down with powdered
milk stirred in tap water. Reboiled,
oversalted canned spinach. "You want
big muscles like Popeye's, don't you?"
And smashed wilted carrots for "20/20 dee-
veesion." Navel oranges, red apples, fingernail
beds of peels. Two slices of paper thin white bread.
"Eat all the food on your plate or you can't go outside
to play. The poor peckin' children are starving in China."

Catholic Death

Her
braids
shiver as she
lights a candle
on the altar to save
Daddy's soul charring
in purgatory Mama and
Grandma say A good father
not a good husband Cheated
on Mama His biker buds say He
picked up his cracked head Got
on his knees Recited the Act of
Contrition Police report states
they found him under the
front tire She fears
God will never
forgive him

Train Station, 1969

The summer I turned ten, my grandparents
took me on my first trip to Mexico.
We caught the train in Mexicali
before the sun rose, and I slept
until our first food stop
somewhere in the Sonoran Desert.

Grandpa followed Grandma down the narrow aisle
to eat lunch in the air-conditioned dining car.
I wanted to fill my panza
with treats at the depot snack bar
and explore a landscape
I'd seen only in Westerns.

The dirt snapped, stung my sandaled feet
as I waded through the heat
toward the small, lone building
surrounded by tan hills
spotted with brittlebush
and cactus that looked like giant aliens.
Two girls my age stood next to the entrance,
begging passengers for money.
A few people tossed a coin.
Most ignored them.

When I reached the girls, they held out
their dirt-smudged hands and sang,
"Por favor, un centavo."
Their shredded dresses
dangled on their skinny bodies.
Their bare feet stood still

on the burning ground.
I spilled all of my change
into the bowls of their palms.

Back in our sleeper car, I looked out the window
to see the hearty meal I thought they'd order—
a hamburger, glass of milk, and chips or a cookie.
They climbed onto stools at the counter.
The server set down two glasses
filled with ice in front of them and poured
a bottle of Coca-Cola into each glass.
Then he served them chocolate bars.
Grins stretched across their faces.

I switched from feeling proud
for sacrificing my lunch money
to being mad at them for buying junk.
"Why the sour face?" Grandma asked
from across our fold-down table.
I explained what happened.
She raised her eyebrows at me.
"And what were you going to buy?"

Man Catchers

Twenty-three, widowed with two little girls
Tradition demanded Mama find a good
Catholic man to take care of us.
Grandma took her to Harris' Department Store,

bought figure enhancing dancing dresses.
No Elizabeth Taylor cleavage cut.
Mama was too dignified, too demure.
Tailored Jackie Kennedy style,

hair and makeup like Natalie Wood's,
she kept her beauty permanent
in a portrait hung on the living room wall.
Mama snagged a husband quick,

tossed those man-catching gowns in the garage.
Perfumed with car oil, dust, I slipped into
a gold lame sheath or a strapless iridescent full skirt.
Tripping in high heeled pumps dyed to match,

I argued with Warren Beatty,
sang West Side Story scenes,
gazed at the stars with James Dean.
Elementary school years filled

dating cinema's best boyfriends
'til I got caught cha-cha-ing
with an air partner. Dorky Derek peeked
through cardboard window covers. Laughed,
said I looked like a circus hobo

and was too old to play dress up.
I ran out to chase him away.
He slammed his mouth into my teeth.

First kiss the same summer Mama
donated the dresses to Goodwill,
made me give my Barbies to little sisters.
We moved to a new town
where I started seventh grade.
No more pretend.

What a Mother Teaches Her Daughters

She wouldn't let her two girls see her
in the morning until she drew on her face
Scolded them to leave the room
whenever she undressed
Concealed her floppy upper arms
with elbow length sleeves

They snuck peeks of her drooping V breasts
the belly shriveled like an overripe orange
and began to understand the purpose
of all the underwear they folded on laundry day:
full body armor girdles, tummy suck-in panties,
mummy-wrap strapped bras

When they reached their teens
she took them into the bathroom
whispered the story about how
the oldest girl was growing inside her
as she spoke her wedding vows
before the cold marble altar

This confession released her from the part
she would never tell them—
her father's belt smacking her,
a fallen daughter,
for the first and last time

The girls learned
that it takes too much elastic,
time, and imagination to conceal
skin a woman should celebrate

The Mexican Jesus sings lead tenor
in the Our Lady of Guadalupe teen choir

The Mexican Jesus is a guy at my church who has dulce de leche skin and looks like the Christ statue flocked with white lilies on Easter morning.

The Mexican Jesus' blue-black, just washed, resurrected-Christ hair hangs free. Grandma says, "It's disgraceful. That boy comes to God's house all greñudo. He should at least pull it back in a ponytail." I point at the long-locked effigy stretched out on the bronze cross floating above the altar and whisper, "What about him?" She digs her fingernails into my thigh and hisses, "Callate l'hocico, diablita." I don't care what she thinks of me; she just insulted my maybe future boyfriend.

The Mexican Jesus is a junior at San Bernardino High and makes straight Bs. When he graduates, he's gonna take classes at the local JC. Patty, my best friend, told me so.

The Mexican Jesus is too old for me. I'm thirteen going on fourteen, but I join the choir for the summer anyway—to be close to him. Mama even lets me take the bus by myself from the bench to the Westside for rehearsals. Otherwise, I'll lie on my stale sheets all day, eating watermelon and running the water cooler. The choir is the answer to her prayers.

The Mexican Jesus doesn't pay attention to Bridgette, Patty's sixteen-year-old sister who has sparkly eyes for him. She keeps her mean eye on me. She's jealous of me ever since the night she thought the cutest boy at the Tomorrowland dance crossed the floor to take her hand but asked for mine instead.

The Mexican Jesus comes to every rehearsal. So do I. The choir rehearses twice a week and sings at the Saturday evening and Sunday afternoon masses. This is more church than I'm used to. Though, I don't feel more holy.

The Mexican Jesus stands in front of me in the choir. When he sings his solo, his arms and bony body tremble like he's walking on water. His head nods up and down fast, making his long hair ripple and swing. He belts out, "Lamb of God, you take away the sins of the world," and I imagine combing his wet hair with my fingers after he steps out of the public pool, his locks spilling into my open hands, splashing my face like a waterfall.

The Mexican Jesus and I stand on the opposite end from Bridgette, who I catch throwing me dirty looks. She knows what I'm thinking.

The Mexican Jesus looks so cute driving his dad's beige Rambler to the choir's fundraisers. We all meet early on Saturday mornings at La Plaza Park to wash cars or sell fireworks. Bridgette and I wear the shortest shorts we're allowed because Patty told us we have the kind of legs boys like. The Mexican Jesus stays too busy talking to customers, counting money to notice us.

The Mexican Jesus and the choir take a bus trip to Oceanside. Strung up in a new pink and brown bikini that Bridgette could never look so good in, I ignore the riptide signs, wade out to the curls to show off my strokes.

A giant wave slaps me, pulls me under, tosses me into forward somersaults, backward somersaults, forward, backward, and finally spits me out on the beach where I land on all fours, tangled in seaweed, gasping. My hair droops over my face like a sandblasted curtain. My skin stings. Sand weighs down my cups, rubs the inside of my mouth. My bottoms are twisted. The breeze tingles my bare butt cheeks. From the corner of my eye, I spot the others in the distance, preparing the bar-b-cue. Relieved that nobody saw me, I suck air deep to keep from sobbing.

"Are you alright?"

The Mexican Jesus is talking to me for the first time! I want to throw myself back in the ocean like a reject-fish.

"Here, take my hand."

The Mexican Jesus *almost* saved me.

The Summer Before 9ᵗʰ Grade

Before I lassoed my first tongue-kiss
and my longhaired boyfriend ignored me
in science class the next day,
before I ran for Valentine's Queen
against my ex-best-friend
and we broke out flailing Chihuahua claws,
yanking hair, yelping cuss words
in front of the principal's office,
I woke to the trill of tin bells,
strapped on two-inch suede platforms,
clonked four and a half long blocks
through heat waves rising from the sidewalks,
held down my neon orange and lime
miniskirt and climbed the bus
headed for the San Bernardino Main Library.

The click and slide of card catalogs
played funkier grooves
than Tower of Power's "Bump City."
Crackling book spines
engraved with golden curlicues
excited me more than a boy-girl pool party.
I couldn't wait to plunge the crinkled pages inside.
All morning, I squeezed hard backs
between Dewey Decimal neighbors,
helped text hunters explore shelves.
Whenever the mean librarian couldn't see me
behind the oversized section,
I snuck a read.

On scorching afternoon rides home,
books pointing out of my backpack
like a fisherman's net after a good day's catch,
I made a pit stop at Esperanza Market
on Mount Vernon Avenue where the butcher
wrapped up a pickled pig's foot for me.
With my legs sweat-stuck to the plastic bench seat,
I gnawed that pata to the bone,
cooled off with Robert Frost's poems.
The bus slanted up Fifth Street to Foothill
while I dove deep into songs of tinkling brooks
and leafless woods until my stop
at the bench on Meridian Avenue.

Christmas Morning

You're waiting for me
in your driveway when I pull up.
Your hands tucked in the pockets
of your gray sweatshirt, you talk to me
through the driver side window
of my yellowing Toyota Corona.
You unwrap my present,
a white porcelain bong.
Your gift for me, an ultimatum:
"Either we go inside and announce
to my family that we're engaged,
or it's over."

Since we started going out when I was sixteen,
this same scene had played in my head:
I'd sit in the pews with our wedding guests
and watch us floating above the altar.
Our Lady of Guadalupe
and San Martín as our witnesses,
we'd promise to stay together por vida.
Last August, on my eighteenth birthday,
you proposed. That night, my fantasy changed.
You lifted my veil. For the first time,
I saw my face. I was twenty-five.

For months, you've taken me shopping
for furniture, stopped at jewelry stores
to try on diamond rings.
I put you off, not sure

how to tell you I wasn't ready.
Yet, I thought you loved me
enough to wait.

I grab the bong from your hand,
slam it on the steering wheel.
Memories shoot through the cold air,
glint in the sunlight
beaming through my windshield—
me, creeping down dark streets
like a stray cat searching for you
those nights you stood me up.
The weekend we spent
at a cheap motel room
hiding my bruised face.
The same motel where we stayed
after concerts, dances, and keggers,
trips to L.A. and Palm Springs.
Our bodies sang like mockingbirds
until dawn put us into a deep sleep.

Silent, you turn your back to me
and head into your house.
I drive north,
toward my town,
toward I don't know where.
I switch on the radio.
As though on cue,
Dave Mason's singing
his hit song about a break up,

"We just disagree."
It's not that simple for me.
I want to be with you
just not the way you need.

I could make a U-turn,
but I keep driving
away from the rest of my life.

The Drive

Mama used to take a shortcut to South San Bernardino when my little sister and I were kids. The first stretch was on Rialto Avenue, a lone road almost a mile long. It reminded me of the empty desert scenes in cowboy movies. On one side was an open field with eucalyptus trees, tumbleweeds, and train tracks. A few houses lined the other side, but we rarely saw anyone outside. There weren't many streetlights, so Mama never drove that route at night.

At the end of the stretch was a steep hill. When Mama reached the edge, she put my dead Daddy's white '61 Impala in neutral and let the car nose-dive down to the bottom. My little sister and I slid forward on the red leather backseat and our stomachs flew up into our ribs.

"Faster, Mama! Faster!" We shrieked long and loud, like the Santa Fe whistle, until we landed on the bottom at Rancho Avenue.

Years later, I was almost nineteen and drove my own car down Rialto Avenue—a brand new gold Toyota Celica with a moonroof. That summer, I gave my girlfriends rides to parties, jams at the park, Newport Beach, and the local mountains. We cranked up my stereo and blew pot smoke out the open moonroof.

The Sun Telegram was running stories about a gang of cholos from San Bernardino who raced their lowriders up and down Rancho Avenue in Colton, the next town over, playing target practice with the gang that hung out at a corner taco stand. Mama told me I had to take the long way to Colton until things cooled down. But the long way added ten minutes to my trip, and cops patrolled those streets. Cruising down Rialto Avenue, I could smoke a joint and blast my music.

Shortly after sundown one sweltering Friday night, I was heading to Colton to see a friend. I decided not to change my route for some pendejo cholos who were fighting a war without a cause. If the Colton gang was stupid enough to keep hanging out where they were getting shot, they deserved what they got.

I floated a wish out the moonroof that the cholos weren't out yet, disobeyed Mama's orders, and hung a left onto the dark wild west of Rialto Avenue.

As I steered into the right lane on the two-lane road, a lifted white pick-up truck swerved around my left side and into the barren on-coming traffic lane. Up until then, I didn't know anyone was behind me. The mini-car hitched onto the back of the truck whipped like a stingray's tail, and almost hit me as the driver jolted in front of my car. Startled, I pulled onto the unpaved shoulder, chalking the air with dirt-dust. The truck growled and took off.

I figured that either I was driving too slow or maybe the driver had too much to drink. Happy hour had just ended at the bars. Lifting my foot off the pedal, I let my speedometer drop so he could get far ahead of me. Instead, he pulled to the side of the road and stopped with the lights on. *He is buzzed,* I thought, *and he's parking until he can see straight.* I kept my eyes on the ten feet of headlight-sprayed road in front of me in case he looked my way as I passed him. I didn't want to encourage him. A hundred pound, five foot, teenage girl driving alone in the wide open might strike a drunken guy as easy prey; the same way a jackrabbit munching on some grass in a clearing looked to a coyote.

Thinking I was safe, I turned the dial to KCAL and rocked out to Van Halen. Seconds later, the truck rammed into my back bumper. My head bobbed like a dashboard chihuahua. By reflex, I twisted the wheel to the left and veered into the empty oncoming car lane. The truck rammed into me again. My car zigzagged across the road as I struggled to stop the wheel from jerking back and forth. I got back into the right lane, and the truck pulled up behind me and switched on the brights. The high beams hit my rear-view mirror and splashed into my eyes, blinding me.

Everything moved so quickly that I didn't think about the danger I might be in. My focus was on getting away. I sped away, and the truck zoomed around my left side, snapping the mini-car in front of me so I couldn't pass. Then the truck slowed down and pulled onto the shoulder, letting me pass, and hovered behind me with his brights on again.

Somehow I caught a glimpse of the driver. It was a white man driving that big white truck. Before I could register what that might mean, he bumped my car from behind again. The edge of the hill was a few feet ahead. I pressed the gas pedal to the floor, and my Celica flew down the hill faster than Mama's Impala ever did. He stayed right on my ass.

At the bottom of the hill, I scanned the parking lot of the liquor store on the corner, hoping someone who could help me was outside. The parking lot was empty. I turned right onto Rancho Avenue, toward the cholos' war zone.

Just as I rounded the corner, the man skirted close to my door. My tires on the passenger side scraped the curb as I tried to keep him from side-swiping me. The chase resumed. I slowed down. He slowed down. I rushed forward. He was on my side.

The cholos' corner wasn't far ahead. I prayed they were perched on the picnic tables outside the taco stand, ready for a fight. When I finally reached the corner, the liquor store, mini-mart, and taco stand all had closed signs hanging in the windows. The welcoming neon lights and electric storefront signs were off. Only the streetlights cut the darkness. There wasn't one bandana-headed ése around. Before I could plan my next move, the white truck smacked the back of my car.

"Who is this asshole!" My mind rambled, trying to figure out who I might have crossed. I hadn't done anything to make someone this mad. The roads were full of Celicas these days. I convinced myself he had mistaken my car for someone else's—

someone he was real mad at. Once he saw I wasn't the person he was after, he'd leave me alone.

I turned off the ignition, flung open my car door, and stomped in front of the spotlight of his high beams and over to the driver side of the truck. Standing on my tiptoes to see into the opened window, I quickly took in his face. He was pale, in his early thirties, and clean-cut with baby smooth cheeks. He looked like a guy I'd feel secure with if he stopped to help me change a flat tire in the middle of nowhere.

"Look, I'm not who you think I am, so just leave me alone."

"I know exactly what you are. You're a dirty Mexican," his said with a slight twang. He gave me a once over, snarling.

His words stunned me. I hadn't considered he'd attacked my car just because I was Mexican. This was my first time experiencing racism. Although I'd heard stories about people getting beat up, it didn't occur to me that I might be in serious danger.

"I'm getting the number off your license plate and reporting you to the police," I yelled in a tattletale rhythm, as though I was scolding one of my little sisters.

"Go ahead," he said, amused. My threat was as meaningless to him as a mosquito he'd smack dead on his arm.

Something inside me took over and walked my body to the back of the truck. He opened his door, and leaned out and watched me, chuckling. No license plate. It was probably in the front, biting my bumper.

"Get away from my truck, you filthy Mexican whore."

I found myself screaming in his face with no idea what I was saying or doing: "How in the fuck can you talk to me like that? This...this...THIS IS AMERICA."

"Don't cuss in front of my wife and child. Don't you have any decency?"

For the first time, I saw the woman sitting beside him in the middle of the bench seat and a little boy about nine or ten, who looked just like the man, sitting beside her. Silent and still, they stared at me like I was crazy. All three of them were blonde and blue eyed. They looked as harmless as the von Trapp family from *The Sound of Music*.

Standing alone on the street, on display in front of the three of them and their disgusted faces, I thought about the clothes I was wearing—a faded black t-shirt and a pair of Levi's scrawled with my red, blue, and green ink drawings of hearts and flowers and the names of my favorite rock bands in wild lettering. With a flick of this man's tongue, my cool-casual-girl style, as my girlfriends called it, became a hideous, sleazy outfit. I felt my breasts protruding through the t-shirt, the round of my hips and butt stretching my jeans.

Do I look like a whore? I wondered. The fluorescent lights above poured over me like a boiling pot of thick mole poblano and prickled my scalp and skin. The realization that a stranger wanted to treat me harshly just because I had brown skin, because I was Mexican, punched me hard in the gut and took my breath.

Cholos, come quick with your bullet and get rid of this man, I silently prayed.

Still on automatic pilot, I quietly walked back to my car, plopped into the driver's seat, shut the door, hugged the steering wheel, and sobbed. The rest was sounds:

Rubber soles pounding asphalt, getting louder as they got closer.

The screeching of the truck backing up.

My car convulsing as the truck released its hold on my bumper.

Adolescent-boy voices shouting, following the direction of the truck's engine as it roared away.

I kept my head down the entire time.

A cholo tapped lightly on my window: "Are you okay?" He spoke tenderly.

My hands trembled as I rolled down the window. Spit and tears drowned each syllable as I stammered that I was fine. With his face so close to mine, I could see kitten-soft black hairs sprouting from the pores on his upper lip. He was probably in high school, maybe junior high. Five or six other cholos his age ran over and crowded behind him, peering at me with concern on their faces. One of them held his right arm across his chest. A small pistol in his right hand flashed from under his Pendleton.

Suddenly aware of how I must look, I combed my hair back with my fingers and wiped my face and nose on the sleeve of my t-shirt.

"I can get you a soda or something," said the boy with the gun.

Another boy offered to take me to his house until I felt better.

I tried to talk, tried to explain, but all I could say was, "I want to go home."

My chest fluttered like a hummingbird. I forced a smile to assure them I was okay and waved goodbye as I drove away.

They waved at me in unison, and I felt relieved and grateful that they hadn't come sooner with their guns, that they didn't get into any trouble, or hurt, or worse. I crossed myself and sent a prayer through my moonroof that the gang war would end.

Everyone was asleep when I got home. The next morning I woke up before Mama and my sisters to check my car. Because of the bumper and door protectors, the wounds didn't show. You had to inspect the back bumper to tell it was pushed in. Mama wouldn't find out I disobeyed her. A few months later, I had to sell the car because I couldn't afford the payments.

So far, I haven't experienced another violent racist attack. I think of that night as an initiation, preparing me for the different types of racism I'd face in years to come—toward me, people I know, and strangers—at work, in public, from friends of friends, strangers, and two boyfriends.

What I'm most grateful for is that my heart opened to gang members that night. I'm only sorry it took me so long to see myself in them and them in me. They deserve the same compassion and understanding those boys showed me.

Still a Young Man

We cruised cool in your jade
'67 Firebird. All wax and buff gleam
beneath E Street lights.
Strapless satin dress and rhinestone platforms,
I side-saddled the middle hump,
told you to pull over quick.
Nachos and tequila sunrises
gushed out of my mouth,
dripped down your custom leather seats.
You stopped and wiped,
whispered, "It's alright,"
while I crouched in the gutter
reddened by brake lights.

Another night, so high
I curled in the back seat.
Parked beneath wide leafed trees,
you and Randy disappeared
through the branches of my sleep.
Fast paced soles
stomping asphalt woke me.
Brown paper sacks and ski masks
jumped in the car. Your engine
hit the highest speeds.
Mama made me tell the cops
you held-up Circle K.
She worked in a courtroom.

We didn't stay in touch much
after you got out of juvie.
The last keg drained at Granger's Hall,

and we frenched in the parking lot.

Inside Taco Tia, you slurred a story
about how Our Lady of Guadalupe
didn't crumble
when you dragged your scabby arms
to mass that Sunday.
Accused me of thinking I'm too good
when I said I don't like drugs no more.

Three years rolled and your ex-
girlfriend's on the phone.
Said you couldn't get off the horse,
waited 'til no one was home,
blasted the shot in the closet.
Took out clothes and stuff first.

I skipped the funeral.
Told myself you left town.

Some gal from your high school
sang Tower of Power's
"You're Still a Young Man"
at Steak 'n Stuff one Friday night.
The time my girls and I
dedicated that song to you on the radio
flashed in my head.
I stepped up to the stage, all smiles,
told her, "Hey, you know Danny?
He's my friend."

"Danny C?" She looked me in the eye.
"Man, he's dead."

Tucker was the finest

country western dancer
in all Yucaipa.
Every Friday night
we made the rounds
in his lifted Chevy pick-up:
Steak Eaters,
Steak n' Stuff,
Steak 'n Brew.
That boy shuffled boards
corner to corner,
his ox-blood cowboy boots
buffed and blinding.
The only guy I knew
who could out-step me,
leave me breathless.
A gringo at that.

My White Russian days.
He ordered Cognac.
Said he learned to sip it
while stationed in Germany.
Served four years then flew back
to Tucker ranch,
seven brothers, ma, and dad.
Postman by occupation,
roper on weekends.
He roped cattle at San Bernardino
and Riverside County rodeos.
Every Sunday morning,
no matter how sore and hungover,
he knelt with his family at Saint Cabrini's.

One of the best boyfriends I ever had.
Always picked me up on time, opened doors,
and paid for dinner and drinks.
Never cheated or played games.
I didn't mind when gals asked me
if they could borrow him for a song.
Still, I had to let him go.
He wanted a good-Catholic-girl wife
who'd give him lots of Tucker sons,
and I wanted to keep
sprinkling my sweat on dance floors.

Standing Tall

"Liz, come here please," Grandma called to me in the kitchen where I was mopping the linoleum with the balding gray-haired mop she'd had for years. It was late afternoon, and I was helping her clean house, coming through on the promise I made weeks earlier.

I quickly leaned the mop stick on the kitchen counter and ran to her side. "Yeah?"

She was cradled in her love seat, taking a break from housework. She wore a frayed cotton house dress, no makeup, and her hair, dyed raven black, was messy. Except for the females closest to her in the family, nobody ever saw her in this state. Grandma fixed herself up before someone visited.

The people in her old neighborhood began calling Grandma a beauty when, at fourteen, she walked through the doors of Our Lady of Guadalupe church one Sunday morning with Mary Pickford curls, red cupid bow lips, rouged cheeks, a petal pink dress with a silk sash tied around the hips, and three-inch heels. Grandma said she loved to wear heels because they made her look tall, slim, and long legged. She wore heels everyday—to work in her family market; to walk five blocks to the soda fountain for clandestine visits with her beau, my Grandpa; and to dance at the church jamaicas and at Columbus Hall long after she married Grandpa and had children. Now 77, she wore comfort shoes and thick support hose.

Her high-heel-mangled feet rested on the arm of the loveseat in front of a novela shouting from the T.V. She turned to me and slowly took me in, from head to toe. In a serious voice, as though someone just died, she asked, "How tall are you?"

"Um, five feet one and three quarters. Why?"

"How tall am I? Five foot two?" Grandma searched the empty space above my head with her eyes, as though I'd hidden some of her height there.

I was the shortest of the adult women in my family, but I'd passed up Grandma years earlier. Still, since her last birthday, she insisted she was taller than me. I opened my mouth to tell her how ridiculous she was when my sister Cynthia walked in the front door, stopping by after work. She took after Grandma and was dressed in a peach business skirt and jacket with matching peach pumps. Her makeup, which she got for free working on the side as an Avon lady, was flawlessly applied to highlight her beauty.

Cynthia kissed us hello, and Grandma soon confronted her for the truth:

"Who's taller, me or Liz?"

"I don't know," Cynthia shrugged. "Why don't you stand back to back and I'll measure the difference between you two?"

"Great idea," I said. She was Grandma's pet. Grandma would believe her when she said I was taller, and the argument would finally be settled.

Wobbly Grandma, with one steel knee, the other plastic, and perennially aching bunions and corns, rushed to the center of the room and posed like a luchador ready to take down a menacing opponent. She stared me in the eye, challenging me to join her.

I strolled over, confident, stood back to back with her, and pressed my flat, limp hair against her beehive—her hairstyle since the forties.

"Remember," I told Cynthia. "Grandma's chongo adds a couple of inches."

"She knows," Grandma scolded me. "Be quiet so she can concentrate."

Grandma and I stood still and straight, our backs pressed together, willing our bodies to stretch to the popcorn ceiling.

"Hmmm," Cynthia said, patting our crowns. She pressed on our shoulders, stepped away from us, and studied the space above our heads. Another, "Hmmm."

"I still need to finish my chores, you know," I said.

"Shshsh," Grandma said.

Cynthia eyeballed our scalps one last time and announced, "Okay, I'm done."

We both faced her, quiet, awaiting the verdict.

"Liz is this much taller than you." Cynthia made a space about three inches between her hands.

"You're wearing heels!" Grandma pointed accusingly at my thin-soled t-strap sandals.

"These are flats." I lifted my feet toward the tip of her crooked air-jabbing finger to prove it. "You're the one wearing heels."

She looked down at her hot pink velvet slippers and their one-inch wedge heels and laughed her chubby laugh, "Oh yeah, I forgot." Then she raised her eyebrows at me. "But, I'm still taller than you."

I opened my mouth and took a deep breath, preparing to argue. Then, I realized that for some reason I couldn't understand, being taller than the shortest woman in the family meant she was still a beauty. I could spare a few inches to bring her joy.

From the time Cynthia and I were infants until Cynthia was nine and I was eleven, Grandma took care of us on weekdays while Mama was away at work. Grandma nursed us when we were sick, taught us how to make Mexican food, danced with us in the kitchen, and always let us know we were loved. She was our second mother. Letting her be taller was the least I could do for her.

"Just a little bit," I said. I held up my hand and made an inch gap between my pincer fingers.

All three of us laughed hearty belly laughs.

Sleeping at the Bottom of Minnesota Street, Lincoln Heights

On my evening jog, I puff up Holgate Square to watch the cute, white med students bolt behind triple-lock doors. Latina and Asian mamas hand their children tortilla strips and small white rice balls to toss to the ducks as I navigate Lincoln Park's crowded dirt curves. East Lake Boyz rule Flat Top's backside. Spray paint, glass slivers, and bullet shells glitter the road. Pit bulls lounge on the yellow line, throw dirty looks at passersby. I take a detour.

**

"For 24 hours I won't speak to you," Libby, my housemate, warned me in advance so I wouldn't take it personal. "Every Yom Kippur I stop making noise so I can hear myself." This holiday of atonement is the only Jewish ritual she observes. For almost a year, I've sublet the revamped two-room basement beneath her.

Upstairs, Libby ends her silence by tinkling a new composition on out of tune piano keys. The melody harmonizes with the next-door neighbors' Cantonese chatter and drifts me to sleep.

Under the street lamp outside my front window, a couple who met inside shot glasses crack the quiet night. Their slushy tongues slobber onto my dreams. I flip on the lights, hoping they'll get the hint they're bothering someone. They stumble through the bushes, fall onto the patio beneath my bedroom window, and moan louder and louder. Her squeals drown out my calls to shut up. Finally finished, they crawl under the clothesline with their jeans down around their ankles, and snore.

My mind floats from pictures of their sex to the pelicula behind my eyelids when cowboy boots stomp the cement below. It's screamer gal's old man. He grabs the dude by his collar, lifts him over his head, and slams his back on the picnic table. Next, he cradles the woman in his arms and dumps her in a trashcan. The viejo trips on a rock, teeters back and forth, and lands on his head. While he groans on the ground, the couple unravel onto their feet and dart off in opposite directions. The viejo wobbles down the hill, grumbling in Spanish. At last, peace.

***

Libby sneaks some of my chocolate covered espresso beans from the refrigerator. Only four or five at a time so I won't notice. But I can tell by the sound of the beans rolling like marbles at the bottom of the plastic container.

***

Tools clank in the brick garage on the hilltop where teen carjackers dissect Chevys and Buicks. Around midnight, a flaming, tireless metal carcass shrieks down the asphalt. A loud thud jolts me out of bed. My phone rings: "It's Libby. Come up to the kitchen."

Wrapped in our robes, shivering from the cold, Libby and I peek between curtain slits. All three generations of the Vietnamese family who lives uphill next door scurry around their driveway and sidewalk in their pajamas, like ants that just had their path blocked. A '64 Impala is parked in the middle of their master bedroom.

Fire trucks and police cars flash red on our walls until four in the morning. The elders, still dressed for bed, bang hammers and plywood at dawn and erase the wound by afternoon. The kids, too young for school, crouch in a circle on their concrete front yard, murmuring curled syllables, poking a limp calico kitten with twigs.

***

Inside the fridge, I find a new package of chocolate covered espresso beans. A Post-it note stuck to the lid: "For you" written in red.

***

The scratching sound outside my bedroom window interrupts my nap break between classes at Cal State LA. A SWAT man in his G.I. Joe clothes is crawling on his forearms toward the house downhill next door.

Uniforms pound on doors. Heroin dealers a house away have a bank robber stashed in their attic. The neighborhood is evacuated out of cross fire. Helicopters sound like they're going to land on my roof as I pack clothes and the envelope with a lock of my dead father's hair.

After an overnight barricade, police chop their way into the attic only to find crumbling bird nests and rat carcasses— the suspect's long gone. We're allowed back in our homes. The smell of tear gas lingers in the air as I put away my toothbrush and nightshirt. The clonk of Libby's heels on the hardwood above my head assures me life is returned to regular.

***

Through my front room window, I watch the haze hovering around downtown high rises turn sherbet pink. The fridge door squeaks open and Libby pilfers a couple of beans. They tap against each other as they shift and settle in the container. She's still crunching when she answers my ring. "Let's take a walk to King Taco." Carne asada burritos and horchata, our comida de poder.

***

The rhythm of the cruisers' bass thump gets me running faster. I sprint up Johnston Street, whiz by screen doors steeped with scents of refried frijoles and incense. Mr. Chang tugs a mermaid piñata for birthday-cake-smeared kids. Teens in the Rodriguez driveway show off their hip hop moves. My rubber thighs propel past red and gold garnished houses, aiming for my mattress.

Confessions of a Pseudo-Chicana

Forgive me Our Lady Virgin of Guadalupe
for I have offended you.
It has been eight months
since I lit a votive
or ate a bowl of menudo.
These are my sins:

I refused to taste hot chili until I was18. Mama raised us
on Hamburger Helper and Macaroni & Cheese.
She never even made a pot of beans.

I learned how to make tortillas
from Mrs. MacDougall in home ec.
Mama still uses the recipe.

In high school, I bonged with Allman Brother look-alikes
and rocked out to Lynyrd Skynyrd
more than I suavecitoed to Malo and El Chicano.

After dancing at forty-nine Mexican weddings, I still
don't know what the lyrics to "Sabor a Mí" mean.
(I can't even speak fluent Spanglish.)

My biggest sin of all—
I ate grapes during the boycott.
But Mama made me.

Forgive me Madre Maria. I was brought up
by a mama who thought Chicano was a dirty word,
and a grandma who claims she's *I*-talian.

Keep me from turning into a vendida
with blue contacts, and help me to be
more Chicana! than coconut.

No matter how pochafied I've become,
I will never forget that great-grandpas' sweat
glistens on the metal of Santa Fe railroad tracks;

good ole boys brand and corral cousins
like cattle they own and slaughter;

ninas stitch arthritis into their fingers
inside maquiladoras;

tios' skin, eyes, lungs
get fumigated with pesticides every day.

Madre Maria, instead of kindling
candles with your image to look cool
I'll light the wicks in remembrance of them.

Menudo vs. Hot Dogs

Eeeeuw!
When you bite the tripe
does it slime your tongue?
How can *that*
help your cold,
your hangover,
your stomach flu?
Watching you eat makes me
want to throw up.

Quips from the uninitiated
as menudo squiggles off the spoon
and slurps through my lips.

These same people charcoal hot dogs
for a Sunday pool party.
Stretch cheeks
scarfing down Dodger dogs.

Menudo is all natural.
Simple with 5 ingredients:
hominy, tripe, chili, water,
and salt to taste.
Nothing to hide.
You see it all
float in the bowl.

Wieners got some stuff
you can't find in a dictionary.
Pumped up

with red dye and nitrates.
Carcass scraps
the butcher threw out. Pieces
vultures wouldn't munch.

I'll take that soup
speckled with the lining
of cows' stomachs over
a bunned weenie any day.

Jovencitos and Viejos Circle Her

Their hands reaching out in request
Cumbia? Salsa?
A little cha-cha-cha?

She rules the Crescendo dance hall
Down with more than moves
She's got attitude
That never-make-eye-contact
head swivel,
adamant right arm v slope,
and hips—
chiquito swish side to side
Her body whispers a secret

The other mujeres sit
and watch
and wait
as she twirls by in gold
flecked pink chiffon
Puts family women to shame
Pray they'll look so good
when they reach 83
with knee arthritis

Her chongo remains
raven black
She sways floor-boards
'til the band's
last cumbia

Go girl, Grandma

49

Songs for First Dates

Try writing a piece where you start with a command/invitation.
Variation: What about a negative imperative?
     —Stephanie Barbé Hammer, Poet-try Winter 2016
       via Inlandia Institute

Tom, the theater manager
"Don't stand so close to me"
That boil on your neck
is as big as Frankenstein's bolts
and ready to burst
You could have covered it up
with a turtleneck
at least popped your collar
It's cold enough
No, I don't want spaghetti
with red sauce
Please don't order anything
creamy, red or white

Ben, the attorney
"Don't stop believin'"
we're wrong for each other
for more reasons
than because I'm a shiksa—
like I told you
not to visit me at work,
like you insisted
on parking in the lot
and punctured your tires
when pulling into the exit,
like you're threatening
to sue my employer,
like after all that,

50

you expect me to go Dutch

Jeff, my boss's son
"Don't let me be misunderstood"
Just because it's Valentine's
Just because you gave me red roses
and a huge heart-shaped box of chocolates
Just because you bought me
an expensive steak dinner
I won't let you kiss me
Your father asked me
to go out with you,
give you a try
I did
Good night

Joe, one of my high school crushes
"Don't stop me now"
Bubbles gurgle in my throat,
threaten to blurt a burp
as we french on my front porch
I waited so long for this date
How I wish
I never drank lemon lime soda
How I wish I could step inside
and let a loud gust loose
The noise might wake up Mama
and our make out session will be over

George, a surprise date
"Don't let the sun go down on me"
Don't let this day end!

The summer hike
to Bonita Falls in Lytle Creek
The cutest boy in high school
The joint of good stuff
His homemade picnic—
even brought a bottle of wine,
and plastic champagne glasses
The kiss sweet and refreshing
as our dip in the stream
We are on the uphill trail of adulthood
where the forest and desert collide
One of the best first dates of my life

Suspension

Solitary tar finger branches drip
Japanese purple petal strokes
I cannot appreciate

Translucent poetry
concealed in cherry wood and glass,
slatted by sparkling particles

His carmine identity
wisps a rice paper wall
protected from fading by shadow

An orchid diluted by dusk
floats above my sleep
A subtle cloud, quiet like Koji

        Purple petal branches
        drip solitary
        finger strokes

        Translucent cherry wood
        glass, poetry particles
        sparkling

        Carmine wisps
        rice paper shadow
        protected

        Diluted dusk floats
        subtle orchid
        Koji, cloud quiet

Destiny

Lu, a contortionist/ performance artist/ palm reader, read my future to me last night. Gabriela Von Stinson, I doubt it's her real name, an avant-garde composer who lives in the apartment above me here in Lincoln Heights, held a party for her artsy friends. Lu arrived early without an invite. For most of the night she sat outside on the balcony in a Morticia Addams wicker chair, smoking pink and gold cigarettes, her wild, violet hair springing out of her head. One by one, experimental musicians, recycled material installation artists, and phonies, dressed frumpy thrift-store style or L.A.-trendy in overpriced torn jeans and designer shoes, closed the French doors behind them, handed her five bucks, spread their palms beneath her violet contact-tinted eyes, and listened to their destinies.

When it was my turn, I told her to check out my romance line. I've been lonely lately. The last time I met a guy who could keep me listening longer than five minutes was six months ago, and he turned out to be a liar.

Lu held my writing hand. Her turquoise nail polish stood out against her pale, freckled skin. The tiny palm trees painted on her thumbnails waved back and forth as she quickly rubbed her thumbs on my palm. After a minute of rubbing, she lifted my now warm, moist palm under the heat of the yellow light bulb in the lamp on the table between us. Taking a drag on her cigarette now and then, she studied my money line and lifeline. She said I wouldn't be rich, but I wouldn't be poor, and I'd live a moderately healthy life until at least eighty. Then she got to my love line.

"You're going to meet the love of your life when you're in your forties. You'll have dual careers at that time too." She leaned in close to me. Musty fabric and b.o. smells wafted from her vintage blue satin mandarin dress. In a serious voice, she said,

"Wait until then to get married, or you'll change the course of your path."

I wanted to ask her more, to find out what she meant by dual careers, but a crowd had gathered in the living room, waiting to see her. So, I stepped back into the party, worried I would have to wait 'til I got married to have sex again. I wouldn't be forty for another ten years.

***

Two months ago, I went to see a psychic who lives four blocks from my apartment. Every day on my way to my bank teller job downtown, I drive by her broken-down Victorian house with the paint peeling off the wood siding and a warped front porch. A huge white sign leans against the front wall, "Psychic" sloppily hand-painted on it in bright red capital letters. The avant-garde composer told me she heard the psychic is a woman who specializes in love spells. I wanted to pay her a visit, but I put it off since I didn't know anyone who had actually seen her.

On one of those unusually smog-free, blue sky Saturday mornings in Lincoln Heights, I couldn't face eating breakfast in bed alone again and decided to trek the hills in my neighborhood and find out if the psychic had a love spell for me. I figured I'd tried everything else—online dating, blind dates, and sitting for hours at a café pretending to read a heady novel by a famous foreign author whose name I couldn't pronounce, hoping a cool guy would approach me. It was time to try a new strategy. And I wanted to find out how she cast spells.

The screen door rattled like it was going to fall off when I knocked on the splintered wooden frame. A tiny blur appeared on the other side of the black-sooted screen.

"I'm looking for the psychic," I said.

"I am the psychic," a high-pitched voice replied. A bony girl who resembled a life-sized doll opened the screen door. She couldn't have been older than sixteen. I wondered if she was for real. The only psychics I'd seen were old ladies in movies.

I stepped inside and caught a glimpse of her right side. The skin on her cheek, arm, and hand looked like melted wax. I crossed my arms and squeezed them to keep from cringing.

"Follow me." She slowly stepped toward the back of the house. She wore a plain, loose brown dress that hung to her ankles and shuffled in beat-up men's slippers. A thick, long dark brown braid swung across her narrow back.

I followed her through the bare entryway, down a hall. The stench of stale air, rotten wood, and urine hit my nose, and I breathed through my mouth. Sunlight snuck through the dirty windows and shined slivers of light on the ripped and yellowed wallpaper. We kicked up dust bunnies and faded confetti as we stepped across the scuffed, grimy hardwood floor. The place was completely silent; I couldn't even hear sounds from the busy street outside.

She led me into a bedroom that was empty except for an altar that took up an entire wall, ceiling to floor, corner to corner. Lit candles, chipped ceramic saints, rusted coffee cans filled with yellow and pink roses, and crumpled photos of sick or dead loved ones left behind by people who had visited before me cluttered the altar. The psychic rushed over to one of the shelves and picked up a picture that fell face down. Smells of burning dust, melting wax, and wilting flowers stifled the air.

About a hundred candles flickered from red and blue votives, brass candleholders, and coffee mugs labeled with business logos such as Clinica de Mujeres, Wu Chan Funeral Directors, Chi Massage School, and Barbarossa Brokers. Sparks crackled and burst from the altar, as though the flames wanted to shoot out and catch on something. Instinctively, I pulled my long hair back in a ponytail.

The psychic stood in front of the altar with her head bowed and hands clasped, praying to a black Virgin Mary the size of a Barbie doll. I hung out in the doorway, away from the fire, waiting for her instructions.

I wondered how she could keep her crinkled skin so close to the altar of fire. The flames calmed down and stopped bouncing from the wicks, as though she had somehow stilled them. She startled me when she called me to her side, the burned side. Curious and a little spooked about what might happen next, I joined her.

"Why did you come here today?" she said, without any feeling in her voice, keeping her eyes on the Black Virgin.

"I want a spell that will bring me a man." I wasn't embarrassed. She probably saw people who wanted love spells every day.

"It'll be forty dollars, twenty now and twenty when you come back," she said in a business-is-business manner.

"Okay." I wasn't sure if I wanted to come back, but I could afford to give up twenty bucks to find out about her spell. And from the looks of her house, she needed the money. I pulled my wallet out of the back pocket of my jeans and handed her the cash.

"You must follow these directions exactly and in the order I wrote them, or it won't work," she said in the same business deal voice. Using her melted hand, she picked up a broken pencil and a scrap of paper from a shelf on the altar and rapidly scrawled some words.

Orange light splashed across our faces as she held the paper out to the Black Virgin, like an offering, and said the directions aloud.

"For seven days, save the water that runs off your breasts when you shower. Return here at dusk on the eighth day. We'll light a candle below the saint of love's toes." She pointed at a chipped and cracked cherub in robes. "I'll pour the water you bring into the flower cans and pray, face down on the floor, until sunrise." She lay down, the front of her body flat against the filthy floor, her right cheek pressed to the ground, and spread her arms out like wings in flight, or Jesus on the cross, and continued to describe the procedure. Her voice squeaked more than before, as though the turn of her neck had twisted her vocal cords.

Within two weeks, a man I could tolerate enough to fall in love with was supposed to appear at my job. I didn't know if I'd go through with it. I still wasn't sure if she was for real, and she scared me. If she was for real, I could be messing with "the course of my path," like Lu said. But I told the psychic I'd be back. She handed me a clean, empty glass nopales jar and said I must use it for the water. She also instructed me to bring a new twenty-dollar bill when I returned.

I had planned to walk downhill to one of my favorite Mexican or Chinese restaurants on Broadway after my visit to the psychic, but after all that trippiness, I headed to the drug store for a chocolate chip ice cream cone. I jogged to de-stress and remembered one of the crazy stories my next-door neighbor Mrs. Talks-Too-Much told me about a friend of hers by the name of Señora Rosales. When she was young, Señora Rosales eloped with an older man who turned out to be a drunk. Every night Señora Rosales stomped over to the corner bar to pull him off some woman's neck and drag him out. After a few years, she got fed up and paid for a curandera to put a spell on him so he'd stay home. The curandera instructed her to clip off some of his pubic hair, collect his earwax on the tip of her bobby pin, and wrap them up with her wedding band in a pair of his boxers. She also told her to bring a bottle of his favorite brand of beer.

Señora Rosales returned to the curandera's with the items the next morning. They spread out the boxers with everything inside in the curandera's cactus garden. The curandera bent down on her knees and chanted the rosary over them. Next, she chugged the beer and poured an herbal solution inside the bottle, dropped the hair and wax inside, and swirled the mix. The woman had to swallow the brew without taking a breath. The curandera

58

told Señora Rosales to go home and her husband would be in his easy chair waiting for her.

She found him slouched in the chair, passed out. While she was gone, he had suffered a stroke and sat there for two hours without any help. He ended up like a baby and Señora Rosales spent the following forty years taking care of him.

Mrs. Talks-Too-Much is always telling me wild stories I half-believe, but now I worried Señora Rosales's story might be true. The nopales jar grew hot in my hand like it had a bad vibe or was cursed. I got scared I might have jinxed my future just by going to see the psychic.

When I reached the store, I went around to the back and threw the jar into an empty dumpster. Loud shattering glass sounds shot out from the bin, like it had exploded. I darted inside the drug store and ordered a triple scoop of chocolate chip. I took a big lick of the ice cream to calm down and vowed to never go back to see the psychic.

***

This morning, alone in bed again with a plate of homemade pancakes smothered with real maple syrup and chopped strawberries and nobody to share them with, I replay the second conversation I had with Lu in my head. Late last night, I was alone in Gabriela's kitchen, where I'd fled to escape two guys who wouldn't stop talking to me about some supposedly cutting-edge European sound artist who tape-records the insides of eggshells. I was pouring a pineapple kiwi cocktail out of the blender when Lu walked in. She stood beside me and poured herself a glass of water. Her skin looked paler, more wrinkled in the glare of the kitchen light. She took a gulp of water and then held her opened hand in front of me.

"A year ago, the doctor told me I had to have a liver transplant or I wouldn't live much longer. My lifeline was cut in half." She dragged her acrylic fingernail in the crevice of a pink root on her palm. "Last month I discovered my lifeline had extended. I went back to the doctor and all my tests came out negative. It's as though I was never sick."

Lu dug through her purse, pulled out a small stack of business cards, and placed them on the counter in front of me. "The lines on a palm change every ten months," she said before leaving the room.

I picked up a card. It had a hand-drawn palm tree in the center. I grabbed two more and stuck them in my back pocket.

I bite into the last strawberry on my plate and think about seeing Lu for another reading. No spells are involved in palm reading. And Lu is for real.

Who knows? In ten months, something much better than a man might show up in my hand.

Sinner

I know you're out there
swallowing Phelan dust.
Driving the I-15 south,
the scent of burnt weeds,
scorched Joshua trees
seeps through my vents.

I could take the Oak Hills off-ramp
Crunch dirt 'til the stake
to your mobile home appears.
Would your brother know why I'm there
and turn the bolt?

If you convert,
I'll pick you up at Union Station,
sail 10 West above the city
to the edge of the freeway.
Glazed with sand and salt water,
I'll crawl onto your breastbone,
nestle in the space between
inhales and heart beats.

Diving into the sooted
sky of Cajon Pass,
I think of you
flamencoing guitar strings,
antiperspirant chalking
your armpit hairs, eyelashes
kissing my inner thighs. How

I long to watch you dream
and smell your pine soap on my pillow.
You save yourself,
cramped on a single bed
surrounded by splintering
wood panel and singed air.
Your crucifix
nailed above your head.

September Reds

for Rachel

His smile wanes
in the medicine cabinet
beside a bottle of morphine tablets
that no longer muffle his pain

Hours trickle through a tube
His mind rambles, stops on a thought
then spins 100 warped syllables:
he hasn't raked the leaves in weeks
a memo to Gruber & Glickstein
Will not return to the office

One lung can't expand enough
to let the death sounds loose
He hates the chit-chat of visitors
the human bedposts' rerun of,
"How do you feel?"
Like shit

Outside the window,
a collage of red and orange
bursts into hummingbird wings
They lift him
out of the rented hospital bed,
up the stairs
and tuck him in his wife's arms

He doesn't want to die
just yet
      but soon

The Summer the Women Stayed Indoors

East Bay, 1997

Even those without air conditioning
kept their windows latched, doors bolt-
locked and chained. They sweat it out.

Only do errands during daylight.

The rapist broke the m.o. of his kind,
struck during the afternoon in wide open
public spaces. No type: Any color,
any age, any size. Any woman.

*Be aware of locations where rape
is more likely to occur and avoid them.*

He grabbed one woman walking
on a busy Berkeley sidewalk.

*Remember, you are not trying to fight the attacker;
you are looking for a way to escape.*

The temperatures rose,
and women were holed up in hospitals
sucking their dinners through wired jaws.

*Whatever you do, don't let him
take you to another location.*

Walking her big dog on a crowded path
(she took all the precautions),
a woman got trapped in a lapse of people.

He was waiting for her.
The dog yelped, caught on the leash.

Don't yell the word help;
people will ignore your call
Yell fire or 911.

An afternoon in the soundproof
music room at a local college,
practicing the piano, her back to the door.
She didn't hear him.

Avoid exercising outdoors after dark.

That summer I stopped
taking walks alone.
Like a child stuck at home with the flu,
I stood behind the window
and watched with envy
as a neighbor man ran by
shirtless, wearing short jogging shorts.
He crossed the street
without bothering to look both ways.

Isolation

For women prisoners in the Andes, Peru

glow of moon smudges
pitch sky

steel clouds shoot
ice bullets into her
concrete cell

her body, shrouded
by a thin
blood-stained shift

hours to sunrises to
winters to years

frayed pieces of her story
collect in the bottom
drawer of a government
official's filing cabinet

want, walk
rest, live

cacophony of syllables
and footsteps
engulf her ears

she learns
how to get a scarf,
a blanket, warm water

tiny gold bells flutter
from the ceiling

can she dream
strong enough to drift
beyond the barbed wire

where cherry red leaves
shudder in moonlight?

Excavating My Father

The sunlight begins to creep through the cloud-congested night as I finish drawing the floor plan of the house I lived in until I was three. For the last three months, I've been conducting a writing exercise in my journal to excavate memories that I learned in a creative writing workshop near my studio apartment in West Los Angeles. Recently, memories have been surfacing during the day or in dreams, and I have to draw some in order to capture them.

I filled in the floor plan with yellow, lots of light. That's how it came to me in the dream that woke me at four this morning. I remember I liked to run from the living room, through the hallway, around to the kitchen, and back to the living room. Around and around in a circle.

The front door opened into the living room. To the left, a brown couch upholstered in a material with raised tight loops I liked to run my fingers over sat beneath the picture window that faced the street. To the right of the front door was the hallway to the bedrooms. The first bedroom, on the right, used to be my playroom where I scribbled a border two feet high in a spray of crayon colors on all four walls. When Mama got pregnant with my sister Cynthia, Cindy back then, she and my father painted the room powder pink and put in a crib and chest of drawers. The hallway turned left to get to the center bedroom, my bedroom, also on the right. My stuffed Bugs Bunny stood in the center of my twin bed. My parents' bedroom was at the end of the hall. It got as bright and hot as a sun porch when the curtains were left open on the window that faced the backyard. The hallway turned left again to enter the doorway to the kitchen. Mama would stand in front of the large rectangle window, decorated with white ruffled curtains, and wash dishes while keeping an eye on me as I played on my swing set in the backyard. At the end of the kitchen was the dining area. A left turn, and I was back in the living room. This house, near the San Bernardino and Colton borders in Southern California, is where I experienced my first major heartbreak.

I use my pincer fingers to grab for crayons and coins under the couch cushions when a green and white pack of cigarettes tumbles onto the beige carpet. I push it beneath the couch as far as my arm will stretch. Something inside tells me to hide them before Mama sees.

Although Mama's retired now, she still starts her day before the sun floods the Joshua tree and rock landscape that surrounds her high desert home with three-digit heat. She's probably already finished her first cup of coffee and a bowl of bran cereal; it's okay to call. I describe my floor plan and ask if I got it right.

"Everything except the shed in back. It was wooden and stood on the south side. I'm surprised you remember. I haven't thought about that house in a long time."

Over the years, Mama has shared some details with me about my father and our life together before he died, but not much. She doesn't like to talk about her past, so I've learned to wait until she's in the right mood to ask her about my father. Until now, it never occurred to me to ask some questions, and some I didn't feel comfortable asking, bringing up a past that's been buried for over three decades. In recent years, for reasons I don't yet understand, I've mourned the loss of my father, mourned the loss of knowing what it's like to grow up with a father, and I've wanted to learn more about him.

"Did he smoke menthol cigarettes?" I tell her about the pack I found.

"*I* stuck them behind the couch cushions," she says. She sounds annoyed, as though she's living it all over again. "I wanted him to find the cigarettes and think a man visited me while he was out late at those dingy bars with his buddies." She sighs and gets quiet, like she's thinking. "Did I ever tell you the nightmare I had that came true?"

I'm glad she's in a storytelling mood, and I'm eager to get more pieces of my father, even if what I learn hurts. "No, what happened?"

"I was dreaming your dad came home with lipstick on his shirt. I raised my arm to slap him, and the sound of the keys turning in the back door knob woke me up. I turned to the clock on the bed table; the face was lit in green. Three in the morning. I held my breath and listened. He banged into the coffee table, mumbled, and started snoring, getting louder and louder. Barefoot, I quietly tiptoed to the living room. He was passed out on the couch. I clicked on the lamp above his head to see if my nightmare was coming true. Red lipstick streaked the collar I had starched and ironed the day before. I smacked his cheek, hard, and ran back to the bed, pulled up the covers, and waited. He grunted, moved around, and started snoring again. The back of my hand stung for hours."

I never told her, but I knew my father had cheated on Mama. A nosy, curious child, I used to listen in on Mama and Grandma's private conversations when they had sent me away to play. But I don't remember hearing any specific stories, and I didn't ask when I got older. I was fine with leaving the stories vague. If I had to have a father who died when I was three, I needed him to be a good man. The knowledge that he hurt Mama on top of the pain of growing up fatherless was too much for me.

I'm standing on the backseat, driver's side, of Daddy's new Chevy Impala, looking out the side window. My eyes are fixed on the door where he disappeared inside the white building. Finally, after what seems like hours, Daddy opens the passenger door. He's cradling baby sister Cindy in his left forearm and long fingers. I jump out and wrap my arms around Mama, sobbing and smearing mocos on her blouse. Her tummy is still round as a watermelon, and I worry there might be another baby inside. Daddy squats down in front of me so I can say hello to my new baby sister.

It's Saturday, my day off. Even if I had plans, I'd cancel them to hear about my father.

"Your daddy spanked me once because of you. I guess you want to hear that one, too."

"For as long as you feel like talking," I say. I squeeze the handset between my left ear and shoulder and climb down the ship's ladder from the loft where I sleep in my studio apartment. As she talks, I take a pee and prepare my breakfast— coffee and a bowl of cereal.

"When he came home from work, he'd call your name as soon as he stepped in the back door. This afternoon you didn't run out to the kitchen like you always did. I was busy folding towels in my bedroom and told him you were playing with your friends next door. He went outside and called for you over the back fence. Then he rushed into the house, said the kids hadn't seen you all day, and he was going to look for you. His keys jangled like warning bells as he swiped them off the kitchen counter.

"About ten minutes later, he walked through the back door, carrying you in his left arm. He was left-handed. You know that, right?"

"Yes, and so are you and Cynthia. What happened?"

She pauses to take a drink of her third cup of coffee. "He found you two blocks away at the liquor store. You were sitting cross-legged on the counter, eating red licorice, talking cute with the owner, old man Mike." Her voice changes to a scold. "You could have been hit by a car when you crossed busy Rialto Avenue."

"Mom, I was just a kid." Hearing these stories, I better understand why she resists talking about the past.

"Well, so you were," she says. "Your daddy put you down and told you to go to your room and color because he was going to spank mommy for losing you. I thought he was kidding. Your door closed, and he led me to the kitchen table. He sat on a chair, bent me over his lap, and whacked my butt. Just once, but that was enough. It hurt."

Daddy's driving me around the neighborhood on the back of his motorcycle. It's cold. Gray clouds darken the sky, but I'm warm, pressing myself against his back, my hands tucked into the pockets of his leather jacket. He turns down our back alley and steers into our carport. He stops, twists around, and lifts me off the seat. I lock my arms around his neck and let my legs dangle. I beg him to let me go with him. He smiles and kisses me on my lips. "I'm going somewhere little girls can't go."

He rolls the bike backward into the alley and tells me to go inside. I run through the kitchen to the living room, jump on the couch, and stand in front of the window to watch him flash by. His bike roars in the distance long after I can't see him anymore.

"It was after nine o'clock and pitch-black outside when I heard the knock on the front door. I turned on the porch light and peeked out the curtains. I saw the police standing on the front steps and knew something bad had happened to your dad on his bike. After they told me about the accident, I got you girls out of bed and wrapped you in warm clothes. They drove us in the police car to Grandma and Grandpa's. I overheard one of the policemen whisper to Grandma that I was in shock because I didn't cry when they told me your daddy had died.

"I left you with a babysitter, my second cousin, for the rosary, mass, and burial. You were too young to understand a funeral, and I hadn't found a way to tell you about your father."

The phone calls and visitors have stopped. After I finish eating dinner, I step into the living room where Mama is on the couch, sitting straight like she's practicing good posture. She's concentrating on the blank T.V. screen. I stand in front of her so she'll know I'm there.
"Daddy won't come home anymore will he?"
"No, he won't." She pulls me into her chest and we sob.

"That was the first time I cried after your father died."

This news does not surprise me. Mama is not an emotional or affectionate person. But learning that she finally let go and cried with me helps me to better understand our bond. Growing up, Mama was more like a close older sister than a mother.

On November 21, 1962, my father celebrated his twenty-fourth birthday. Mama baked him an angel food cake that fell while in the oven, but she served it anyway. He died that Sunday, four days after his birthday, November 25. At twenty-three, Mama was a widow with two little girls. I turned three a few months before, and Cynthia celebrated her first birthday in early November. She only knows him from photographs and other people's memories.

My father owned two choppers he customized himself. One got destroyed in the accident. The other, I assumed, Mama sold. She doesn't remember. I wish I had a picture of him with one of his bikes. In those days, people didn't take many photographs, but I hope my tios or an old buddy of my father's will find one and think to send it to me and my sister Cynthia.

I learned most of my father's history from my aunt and uncle—his older sister and her husband. He was born in a small town in Chihuahua. His mother, my grandmother, and his father split up when he was a baby, and my grandmother married his stepfather soon after. When he was about nine or ten, my father picked cotton near El Paso, Texas. His family then moved to a strawberry ranch outside Las Cruces, New Mexico, where he did odd jobs. He was about sixteen when he left and drove alone to San Bernardino, where he stayed with friends who helped him get a construction job. By the time he met Mama, he was nineteen and worked full-time as a laborer at Kaiser Steel.

"He'd come home covered in soot and you were so happy to see him I'd have to catch you before you stripped off your clothes and climbed in the shower with him."

Last year Mama gave Cynthia and me copies of the frayed obituary she saved from *The Sun-Telegram*—the local newspaper, his citizenship certificate, and the traffic accident report. The witness statement says my father and three of his biker-buds had taken off from Nuñez Park in San Bernardino and were riding up Fifth Street—also known as Route 66, but we never called it that—on their choppers when my father's biker cap blew off. He made a U-turn, scooped it off the street, and roared his engine to catch up with his friends. A car—the driver was also a young man—was making a left onto Muscott at the same time my father turned around. His bike slammed into the car. The report says the time of the accident was 8:15 p.m. There were no skid marks; the street was too wet. The bike had a dimmed headlight, and no moon or stars shined in the sky.

The details that are important to me I won't ever know. The sound of his voice and laughter, the smell of his neck when he hugged me, the music of his hands thumping his conga, and what he'd look like and be like today.

I lean against the rough plaster outside Johnny Martinez's house, waiting for him to show me to the bathroom. Two of my girlfriends and I are here for his sixteenth birthday party. He takes me inside. It's dark except for bright lights flashing through an open doorway down the skinny hall. I glance in the room as we pass. A small-framed man who looks like he could be Johnny's dad is stretched back in a recliner, mesmerized by the Mexican wrestlers in the ring on T.V. His white tank shirt is hanging out of his blue mechanic's uniform pants. He is holding a coffee cup in one hand. A paper plate full of Mexican food served at the party sits on the table beside the recliner. Something feels familiar about him, but I've never met Johnny's father. Johnny shows me the bathroom door and heads back to the patio. When I finish, I quietly step by the doorway so I won't bother the man.

"Lizzy? Is that you?" The man calls to me.

I stop, frozen, unable to speak. I haven't been called that name since I was a little girl.

He gets up from his chair and walks toward me. "Are you Lizzy Gonzalez, Güero's daughter?"

"Yes, I am." I don't recognize him, but I feel like I know him.

"I rode bikes with your dad. I was with him the night he died. You know, he loved you and your little sister a lot."

I'd heard the last sentiment many times over the years from my Aunt and Uncle and other members of my father's family. Hearing it from my father's friend meant more to me, maybe because I thought Mr. Martinez knew my father better. A few years later, while standing in line for the cash register at a market, I had a similar experience. Another of my father's riding buddies recognized me. He said the same thing, "Your father loved you and your little sister a lot."

"It's after eight," I tell Mama. "We've been on the phone over two hours."

"One more story, and I have to go," Mama says. "J.F.K. was assassinated on November 22, the year after your daddy died. I had sold the house, and we were living with Grandma and Grandpa. During the entire funeral, you and Cindy sat in front of the TV, both in the same position— chins on your knees, arms wrapped around your legs, and the tips of your shoulders stuck to each other's."

I have detailed flashbacks of Kennedy's funeral. While the country mourned him, I mourned my father. Whenever John Junior's famous salute to his father's casket came on the screen, I stopped whatever I was doing and watched. I didn't understand this then, but for me, Kennedy's funeral was my father's funeral, and John Junior saluted my father for me.

It occurs to me that my father and J. F. K. both died at Thanksgiving time, and I look through old calendars I've saved to see what date it fell on those years. Thanksgiving was the day after my father's birthday the year he died, and it came six days after J.F.K.'s death. Neither Mama nor I have memories of Thanksgiving dinner those years. The holiday of gratitude was surely overshadowed by the blow of the deaths.

Hearing Mama's stories is bittersweet. Knowing my father loved Cynthia and me "a lot" isn't as meaningful now that I know how he treated her. Perhaps she kept these stories to herself not only because it made her uncomfortable to share them, but because she wanted to protect me, my father's daughter.

I realize I needed my father to be a hero because my stepfather, whom Mama married when I was five and who left her for another woman eight years later, did not like me.

In some ways, my father is a hero. For someone who grew up impoverished and quit school at a young age, he accomplished a great deal in his short life. His Harley-Davidsons were paid for, and it takes skill to chop a bike, let alone two. He bought the sharp Impala new, and he and

Mama qualified for the mortgage for our house, which had been built only two years before they bought it, without a co-signer. He had a good paying union job and provided for his family. He also conveyed through his actions, not just words, that he loved Cynthia and me "a lot."

Still, to me, a man who treats his children well but not his wife is not a good man. I remind myself he was young when he died. Hopefully, if he had lived, he would have learned to appreciate and value women. Perhaps his love for his daughters would have helped him grow.

My father will forever be a stranger to me, but today we're a little closer.

Haunted

And I will never get used to
your musician's hours
The teeth of your keys
scraping the lock
after the crickets,
exhausted from a night
of high-pitched serenading,
have stopped
Mattress coils whine about
the disturbance of your weight
as you fill the cold space
beside me. Your chest hairs
kiss my spine,
then our tongues fling
icicles aimed to rupture and sting
This is how we sweat together
(Even the sky is ashamed of us)

It is the lack of spoons
and a pot to steam the house
with cooking smells
that keep me hungry
for the ghost of you

Fall in the Chaparral

Santa Ana winds howl
down Cajon Pass

I sleep on the edge
my side of the bed
not to disturb; you
snore on the couch

Gusts plow calico-
hued hillsides

Filigree bones
of a scrub jay's wing
snuggle in the shadow box
you made to save the memory

Flailing yucca swords
slash the moonlight

A battery-operated clock
glows on the mantle
(Electricity is unreliable
during winds and quakes)

Bitter breeze whistles
through window cracks

Your Granny Smiths rot
in the glued-back-together
anniversary bowl
You don't notice the smell

Brittlebush bows
Christmas berry slants, rattles

I scrub pomegranate specks
off the carpet
before you spot them

A coyote crouches
behind beavertail cactus
ready to pounce on a jackrabbit

We waste hours bickering,
like tumbleweeds bouncing
aimlessly in the cactus garden

Dry leaves crumble so easily
veins can't sustain them

Our tromps back and forth
shake the wood floor
startle snakes
slithering beneath the foundation

Manzanita bushes thrash
as though they want to uproot and bolt

We snap our love like weak branches
cracking off eucalyptus trees
You brush shards of us
into a dust pan

Add a spark to the drying landscape
uncontrollable wildfire will result

Flames cleanse the soil
of allelopathic compounds
clear space
for new growth

Buds curl, dry on branches
Cinder does not disintegrate

We toast Thanksgiving
from opposite ends
of our new glass table

Fall quickens

My Valentine

That's it. I dumped him off at the Oakland airport, y chale bro! Have a great time in L.A. with your mommy. There I was, navigating the rain spraying on the windshield like we were driving through a car wash. He blared some experimental music that sounded like car mechanics clanking and clanging out of my speakers, and twisted his face, hollering, "I'm opening up to you! Isn't this what you want?"

I pulled up to the curb of his terminal, and all I wanted was to push him out of the car, fling his backpack and duffel bag at his panza, and head home. Except I didn't want to make a scene in front of all the people at the airport. So I gave him the silent treatment and didn't even kiss him goodbye.

Eight and a half months of the sentido's mood swings, and he says I should at least stay with him 'til Valentine's? He's super-fine, but looks ain't worth all the aggravation. If one of my girlfriends told me a story like ours, I'd say, "Dang, girl, you two need to hang it up."

It's those bee-zarre rituals that make it hard to quit. Four o'clock in the morning, after wangoing on the kitchen table, we'd trade places on the swivel chair and give each other hair trims in the middle of the kitchen in my apartment. We'd check the cuts in the bathroom mirror, smile at each other's reflection, and jump in the shower for another round of sex. I'd get so caught up in the magic I didn't care that I'd eventually end up at Cheap Cuts to straighten out the choppies.

Aaaaay! The sex! It got talkier and more inventive as time went on. I convinced him to speak Spanish while we did it: "Soy tu amor. Mis labios son tuyos. Me gusta tus nalgas, mucho." I had to tell him what to say, and sometimes he forgot. Still, it was better than when we first did it. He didn't make any sounds. I only knew he came 'cause his eyelids quivered and I felt his chorizo shrinking inside me.

I know hot wango isn't a good reason to stay together. But the pool of quality single men is limited for a twenty-three-year-old community college Chicana. Most of the good guys my age are taken. My choices are flabby divorcees who hate their ex-wives or a jovencito Chicano who's a sophomore at Cal and needs some training. Except he's a mama's boy, and his light-skinned Mexican mama claims she's Spanish only and check-marks "white" on the census.

Two months after dating, he asked me to be his girlfriend. I said yes, and three body-slamming hours later, as I lay on top of him, running my fingertip around his belly button, he told me his mama was flying out from LA to visit her mijo for the weekend. I thought he was going to invite me to meet her. No, he asked me not to drop by his dorm or even text him. I felt like my chest was being crushed like chiles in a molcajete, and I broke down crying: "You're embarrassed of me because I'm older than you, because I'm not smart enough to get into Cal, because I'm not güera," and more pitiful lines fell out of me. Sobbing into the pillow, it hit me: *He lets his mama check his texts?* I grabbed his chonies off the floor—tighty-whities his mama probably bought for him— and his dandruff shampoo out of my shower, threw them out the front door, and kicked him out.

Three days later, after he dropped his mama off at the airport, he showed up at my door all sorry. I told him straight: "Do you want to be a boy and suck your Mama's chichi, or do you want to be a man and suck mine? 'Cause you ain't getting any more of me unless you stand up to her." I slammed the door in his face and turned up the volume on the stereo to drown out his knocking. A few hours passed, and he slipped a note under my door that said he had called and told her about me.

I had to know what she said, so I let him in. She asked him how dark I was and if I had an accent. She told him she'd meet me but wouldn't promise to be nice. I had no interest in meeting the vendida. I just wanted her to know about me.

I wonder if we were a boring couple. Some of our best times were when we hunted for a parking spot closest to the used record shops and bookstores on Telegraph or wandered the aisles of Berkeley Bowl, choosing ingredients for the vegetarian concoctions we cooked together. On Sunday afternoons, after making love, we'd sit on the edge of the bed and exchange gifts. He gave me a dressed vela de amor to light every night and keep our love strong, and I gave him a fat dictionary he kept at my place so we could look up words in our school books that we read to each other in bed—words like sarcophagus and truculent.

Maybe we should have one last visit. For closure. There's no reason to leave things on a bad note. Valentine's isn't a big deal to me, but it'll suck to be going through a break-up on that day.

I guess I did overreact when I found out his ex-girlfriend had taught him how to make the veggie omelet he surprised me with this morning, the blonde with a bikini-figure he met in Spain two summers ago, the one his mother keeps a silver framed 8x11 photo of on the piano in her living room, the same photo I took long looks at while he showered that weekend we spent at his mom's when she visited the blonde in Spain.

The dish did taste good. And he made it special for me.

What's a few more weeks? I'll probably need another hair trim by Valentine's anyway.

Espiritu

The voice in the receiver
a crackling memory
of the woman who once wore
hot pink velvet slippers
with a little heel
to clean the house
Telephones hold us close
She says I'm the only one
who calls to check-up on her
(The others stop by)

Death sings from the rusting
rose garden in her front yard
The starched, dustless house
dissolves into gray peeling walls
Clumsy knees
won't let her cumbia
in the kitchen
No broken hips
God blesses her falls
The three dimensional
bleeding Jesus
hangs above her bed
immaculate

Grandma's turned sweet
Soon, the white-winged owl
will light on her windowsill
Ninety-three is closer to finite
If I don't visit
I can look at her old pictures

remember her
the way she remembers herself
Belle of the barrio
The girl with Mary Pickford curls
dancing to the Beer Barrel Polka

At night, she sails a blessing
toward my city
From '63 to '71
she was my mother
Says she can't
keep alive for me forever
But we're not through yet
When she scolds me
I know she's staying
around a while

Fight with me Grandma
Call me diablita
Smack me with your fire

Nunca Means Never

Nellie, Meadowbrook, San Bernardino, 1921

That afternoon, my little brothers and me
were cooling off in the creek
that flowed through our backyard.
I got hungry and ran to the house for a taco.
Climbing the back steps to the kitchen,
I heard Mama telling someone off,
so I tiptoed to the side of the house
and found her alone, with her back to me,
hanging the wash on the line.

"Nunca! Nunca!" she scolded
a bundle of Papa's underpants
and snapped them open, rough.
An explosion of water drops
shot through the air, spraying her.
The braid she wrapped
around her head each morning
glistened like a crown.

"Nunca!" She bent over the tina
filled with clothes she boiled and scrubbed,
shook her head, mumbled in her deep, angry voice,
yanked out a pair of Papa's work pants—
the stains and dirt rubbed away,
jerked them back and forth,
like she was wringing a chicken's neck.

She clipped each end of the waist on the line,
wiped her forehead with her arm,

pulled a rag from the front pocket
of her faded and patched housedress,
blew her nose loud, like a squealing pig,
and stuffed the rag back into its place.

She grabbed Papa's
blue work shirt by the collar.
"I never wanted to live on a farm."
She pinned one shoulder on the line.
"I can't keep the house clean."
She pinned the other shoulder.
"The dust."

She smacked the shirt in the belly
with the back of her hand.
"The flies."
Smack.
"The stinky animals."
Smack.
"Nunca. It's too much work."

Papa's clothes flapped
and swayed in the breeze,
having too much fun to listen to her.

A Mexican Wedding Theme

Grito pink, folklorico purple skin gripping,
chichi poofing bridesmaid gowns
Corrido-orange flores de papeles
bouquets Glittering plaster of Paris
calaca head center pieces
Child scissored, finger painted
paper bag luminarias
Calavera novios waltzing on dark chocolate
cake top to the Beer Barrel Polka

Not to spite your mother
but in spite of her
(She may not show anyway)

What could we add to signify
her German-Argentinean cultura
Milanesa?
            Too expensive
Porcelain cows?
            Ridículo
How about the ushers
snapped up in henchmen uniforms
Tailor the groom general gray
Flap a swastika flag
while the I do's get traded

You say her parents were Jewish
Then why does her talk
sound like Nazi propaganda?

Mama swears the absence
of your mother's hijo único
will chip her stubbornness
Una noche de la familia
she'll appear behind the peephole
arms filled with a pot of puchero
moths and June bugs
hovering around her faded rubia crown
Should I open the latch?

I reserve my bitch tactics
for some pendeja
attempting a lick
beneath your pantalones
Not the woman
who originally
buttoned you into them

¡Vivan Las Mujeres!

Mama, Grandma, a great aunt from San Diego, and an aunt by
    marriage gathered at the kitchen tables of my childhood.
Spoons swirled in lipstick stained coffee cups and ground beef
    tacos crunched as
they planned a daughter's wedding, caught up on family news, and
    whispered secrets in Spanish.
Today, we amigas in the arts hold our own sacred circles at tables
    in homes, cafés, or the library.

Water swirls in lipstick stained recyclable bottles and organic
    crudités are crunched
as we plan arts events, catch up on our personal lives, and listen
    with love to past injuries and inherited prejudices.
We amigas in the arts hold our own sacred circles at tables in
    homes, cafés, or the library.
Into old age, we dig and pave new, nontraditional paths our
    foremothers could not.

We plan arts events, catch up on our personal lives, and listen
    with love to past injuries and inherited prejudices.
Together, our passion for social justice and equity, wisdom, and
    love are amplified.
Into old age, we dig and pave new, nontraditional paths our
    foremothers could not.
We laugh like children during recess, make each other think, and
    revere each other's creativity.

Together, our passion for social justice and equity, wisdom, and
    love are amplified.
The music of elder women's voices planning, catching up, and
    whispering secrets plays in the background.
We laugh like children during recess, make each other think, and
    revere each other's creativity—
lessons we learned from family women's sacred gatherings at the
    kitchen tables of our childhoods.

Fulfilled

Tomorrow, I'll wake up with
tumbleweed-tangle hair
because tonight we are not
the laced and zipped middle-aged couple
we take out of the house
but ourselves in a fog of grunts
wriggles, angles, and curves
Our bodies clasp together—
one pulsing techno groove
A cat licking itself clean We are
synapses sparking
water spouting
out of a whale's blowhole
My skin is the shore
for your tongue tip and teeth
And you, a modern gaucho
I clench your ass with both hands
as we gallop across the mattress
This is when I get so grateful, I promise
to never nag at you again
We finish together
two dirty pigs dripping
the mud of our sweat
Sugary-tart jellies
shimmering the sheets
I run to pee while you
go to the kitchen, pour me
a glass of cranberry juice
Even the practical
is part of our sex   Now
our chests play a tempo

as slow as "Monk's Mood"
We collapse into each other
like boxers at the end
of a fifteen round match

Postcards from Where I Live

Be Thankful for What You Got
  —William DeVaughn, Written and performed

Growling pit bulls and German shepherds
jump spiked gates and crunch Chihuahuas like taquitos
in my North Long Beach neighborhood.
I carry a metal rod, stay on guard while walking Chacho,
my cream and caramel Jack Chi. We avoid certain streets,
circle the same eight-block radius of flat concrete and asphalt.
Whenever we can, we hop in my '95 Toyota Tercel
for an escape just twenty minutes away.

We park at the bottom of Signal Hill, wind up Skyline Drive,
up the gated community's paved paths. I'm breathless;
Chacho's ready to run. We compromise and power walk
around Hilltop Park's rim and Panorama Drive,
pass the squeak of bobbing oil pumps.
Air swept clean by Santa Ana winds
reveals L.A. high rises and San Bernardino mountains.
The cobalt blue pyramid at CSULB rises from treetops.
Huntington Beach's jagged shore shimmers and froths.
Off the Long Beach coast, yachts and freight ships
cruise by artificial islands where palm trees
and happy colored towers camouflage oil pumps.
Behind the Queen Mary, gantry cranes stand erect,
like steel dinosaurs ready to do some heavy lifting.

At White Point Nature Preserve, Chacho pulls the leash
taut on steep foot-carved trails.
Salt and sagebrush scent the breeze.
Battery Bunker's empty gun encasement
frames views of fluttering yellow fennel buds;
cactus wrens feasting on swollen prickly pear;
Catalina Island on a fog free day.
A lone speedboat rips the serene surface.

We stroll down Main Street to the Seal Beach boardwalk.
Barefoot brides in fluffy white tulle and fitted lace dresses
weave through families and couples to make their vows
at Eisenhower park, overlooking the ocean. Lamp posts
lining the wooden pier radiate amber light.
Chacho can't read "No Dogs." He runs unleashed,
kicking up sand smooth as a whisper.

A violet and dragon fruit afterglow saturates the sky.
Chacho and I head back home.
The jazz band is jamming at the PopUPtown
Social outside the local library.
Chacho curls at my feet. Chilling on a tree stump,
I nibble on a vegan tamal, sip a pint of beer,
and give thanks.

Travel by Dragonfly: A Hendrix Infused Poem

Pluck me with your teeth   baby

    Pluck me like

        Jimi Hendrix

           plucks

              his Stratocaster strings

Flick

   your purple flames   until we're an octave

                        fuzz

blazing the bed

      torching the walls

           Sacrifice for our love

Let's lick a riff
so loud
feedback
catapults us
through
the smog-sludged sky

We'll hop
on a dragonfly
arc
over Jupiter's moons

Like starfish,
stroked by Jovian clouds,
"Little Wing"
floats us to Saturn
our love making
in a psychedelic
sea
Baptizes

Your Jam

You didn't know you'd be surrounded by the newer, bouncier
products that delight customers—that you'd stare middle age in
the face and carry its soggy weight for everyone. And yet, you
don't feel ugly or incapable.
            — Antonia Crane, "Your Life as A Middle-Aged Stripper"

You won a hot legs contest
at thirty. A broke late bloomer
completing your BA in Los Angeles.
The only time you entered
a competition based on body parts.
You, horse jockey short
up against two long-legged,
four-inch heeled,
skirts up to their cheeks
veterans in their early twenties. You
sauntered across the dance floor
shaking your body to "Nasty Girl"—
your strapless black satin dress
tight as Vanity Six's in the video,
sat sideways on the lip of the stage,
slowly slipped off
each shiny black pump,
then each stocking.
You carried them in one hand
and salsa-ed away.
Easiest hundred bucks
you ever made.

This year you turned 58.
40, 50, even 55 didn't faze you,
but now you're almost 60.
¡Hijole!
Got an aching click
in your right hip;
a knot in your neck
tugs at your shoulder.
Maybe Black don't crack,
but Brown sags.
You read about a forty-six-year old stripper
who can hang upside down
from the top of the pole
and remind yourself:
You're still bendy.

Your strip song:
"While My Guitar Gently Weeps"—
the tribute performance to George Harrison,
your favorite Beatle.
During his skin tingling guitar solo,
Prince did a back bend
you plan to replicate
while grasping the pole.
You pick a territory you know,
a place with a few booths and a small stage
like Frank Zappa's hangout in Colton
that turned into a titty bar.

No shiny polyester and butt gyrations.
Leave that to the young ones.
Two snaps and your red wrap dress
falls off.
Peekaboo thigh high boots

make up for the one-inch kitten heels.
Gotta watch your back.
Although you could use it,
you probably wouldn't make any money.
Most men don't look at,
let alone tip,
women your age,
especially those like you
who can't rock a g-string.

During your fantasy, you flashback
to after the hot legs contest.
A true college-aged guy
asked if he and his friends
could buy you a drink.
They surrounded you
like some nubile celebrity,
said they voted for you
because you didn't
give it all away.

It wasn't because you're a lady
or modest.
You're not.
Dancing is all your own.
You've been dancing
since before you could walk.
You dance
while doing housework
or grocery shopping.
You're in front of the band
for their first and last songs.
Like Grandma and Mama,
you'll be getting down

when you're an octogenarian
without a care what men think.
Spontaneous,
in the moment,
your spirit and body
rejoice.

You do it for fun,
for no one but yourself.
Your life,
your jam.

NOTES

"Songs for First Dates," p. 49

"Don't stand so close to me" performed by The Police

"Don't stop believin" performed by Journey

"Don't let me be misunderstood" performed by The Animals

"Don't stop me now" performed by Queen

"Don't let the sun go down on me" performed by Elton John

ACKNOWLEDGEMENTS AND GRATITUDE

Grateful acknowledgement is made to the editors of the following publications where these works previously appeared, as is or in earlier versions:

COLLECTION:
Beneath Bone (Manifest Press, 2000) "Fall in the Chaparral,"
    "Haunted," "A Mexican Wedding Theme," "Suspension"

CHAPBOOK:
Edges, Recuerdos, and Clean Underwear (liz gonzález and Momentum
    Press, 1995): "Catholic Death," "Man Catchers," "Menudo vs.
    Hot Dogs," "Jovencitos and viejos circle her"

ANTHOLOGIES:
2016 Writing from Inlandia (The Inlandia Institute, 2016): "Best
    Granddaughter," "Songs for First Dates"
*The Coiled Serpent: Poets Arising from the Cultural Quakes and Shifts of Los
    Angeles* (Tia Chucha Press, 2016): "Buñuelos"
Don't Blame the Ugly Mug: 10 Years of 2 Idiots Peddling Poetry (Tebot
    Bach, 2011): "The Summer Before 9th Grade"
Grand Passion: The Poets of Los Angeles and Beyond (Red Wind Books,
    1995): "Catholic Death"
Inlandia: San Bernardino (The Inlandia Institute, 2018): "Fall in the
    Chaparral"
So Luminous the Wildflowers: An Anthology of California Poets (Tebot
    Bach, 2003): "September Reds"
Voices from Leimert Park Redux: Los Angeles Poetry Anthology (TSEHAI
    Publishers, 2017): "Isolation," "Still a Young Man"
Wide Awake: Poets of Los Angeles and Beyond (Beyond Baroque
    Books/Pacific Coast Poetry Series, 2015): "Confessions of a
    Pseudo-Chicana," "Espiritu," "The Four Food Groups in
    Grandma's Summer Lunches"
Women on the Edge: Fiction by LA Women Writers (New Milford: The
    Toby Press, 2005): "Destiny"

JOURNALS AND OTHER PUBLICATIONS:

Art / Life: "Buñeulos," "Fulfilled"

Arroyo Arts Collective Newsletter: "Sleeping at the Bottom of Minnesota Street, Lincoln Heights"

Askew: "Nunca Means Never"

BorderSenses Literary Magazine: "The Mexican Jesus sings lead tenor in the Our Lady of Guadalupe teen choir"

Brújula 33: "Haunted"

Caguama: "Isolation"

Cider Press Review: "Sinner"

City of Los Angeles 2017 Latino Heritage Month Calendar and Cultural Guide: "She's All That"

City of Los Angeles Latino Heritage Month 2007 Calendar and Cultural Guide: "Confessions of a Pseudo-Chicana"

Comet Magazine #4: "My Valentine"

Cooweescoowee: "The Summer Before 9th Grade"

Cultural Weekly: "The Summer the Women Stayed Indoors"

Heliotrope: "Espiritu"

Lummis Day Souvenir Program: "Buñuelos"

Luna: A Journal of Poetry and Translation: "Confessions of a Pseudo-Chicana"

Plum Ruby Review: "The Drive"

Poetry in the Windows I: "Catholic Guilt"

Poetry in the Windows VI: "The Four Food Groups in Grandma's Summer Lunches"

San Francisco Chronicle: "My Father"

Silver Birch Press: "Buñuelos," "Postcards from Where I Live"

Speechless the Magazine: "Fulfilled"

The Squaw Review: "The Summer the Women Stayed Indoors"

Strongbox: "Buñuelos," "Espiritu," "Fulfilled"

Voices: New Poems of Life and Experience: "Man Catchers

Wild Lemon Project: "Train Station, 1969"

Words in the Windows: "Buñuelos"

Mil Gracias to the following family, friends, writing communities, and organizations who have contributed to this book in different ways over the twenty-five years this book encompasses. If I've forgotten anyone, please accept my apology in advance and know you are appreciated.

To those who helped me with *Dancing in the Santa Ana Winds*:

Frank and Carol Kearns of Los Nietos Press for the gift of this book

ire'ne lara silva, editor, for her keen eye and insights

Olga García Echeverría, Lisa López Smith, Juanita Estella Mantz, Lucy Rodriguez-Hanley, Xochitl-Julisa Bermejo, Lois P. Jones, Art Curim, Jerry Garcia, and Jamie Asaye FitzGerald for their invaluable feedback and friendship

Renee Swindle, Consuelo Flores, Olga García Echeverría, Frankie Hernandez, Frances J. Vasquez, Suzanne Lummis, Levi Romero, and Ruth Nolan for their love, support, and guidance

Everyone who pre-ordered and promoted *Dancing in the Santa Ana Winds*

To Manifest Press Staff, Board, Mary Ganz, Editor, and Barbara Barrigan-Parrilla, Executive Director, for publishing *Beneath Bone*.

To those who gave me helpful feedback on manuscripts with earlier versions of poems in this book, feedback I referred to when working on *Dancing in the Santa Ana Winds*:

Ai (RIP) and the participants in her poetry workshop at Macondo 2008

Ruth Foreman, who generously critiqued a manuscript of earlier versions of poems in this book

To workshops where I presented or generated early drafts of works in this book:

Stephanie Barber and participants, Poet-try Winter 2016 Online via Inlandia Institute; Ruth Foreman and participants, Flow Workshops; Lucille Clifton (RIP), Robert Hass, Galway Kinnell (RIP), Dorianne Laux, Sharon Olds, and participants, 2000 Community of Writers Poetry Workshop; Ray Gonzalez and participants, The Writer in the World: Poetry, Fiction, and Memoir, 2000, University of Minnesota Split Rock Arts Program; Aleida Rodriguez and participants, Poetry Workshop, 2000, Flight of the Mind Summer Workshops for Women; Professors and participants in workshop courses, Mills College Creative Writing and English MFA Program, 1996-1998; Terry Wolverton and participants in Flex Your Writing Muscle Advanced Creative Writing Workshop, 1995-1996, Los Angeles LGBT Center; Interchange 6 Writers Collective, 1995-1996; Bill Mohr and participants, Poetry Workshop, 1994-1995, Beyond Baroque Literary Arts Center; Michelle T. Clinton and participants, Multicultural Feminist Poetry Workshop, 1993, Beyond Baroque Literary Arts Center; and ¿Y Qué Más? Chicana Poetry Collective, 1992-1994, where I began writing poetry

To organizations and centers that have supported me directly and indirectly relevant to this book—as a writer, workshop facilitator, or promoter of literacy and the arts:

UCLA Extension Writers' Program Staff, Nutschell Anne Windsor, Program Representative, Linda Venis (Past) and Charlie Jensen (present), Program Directors; Macondo Writers Workshop and Sandra Cisneros, founder; Michelle Obama Neighborhood Library Staff and Shiloh Moore, Librarian; Uptown Business District Staff and Tasha Hunter, Executive Director; Unheard L.A.—live in Baldwin Park, KPCC-In Person Storytellers, Staff, Jon Cohn, and Ashley Alvarado; Poets & Writers and Jaime Asaye FitzGerald, Director, California Office and Readings & Workshops; Arts Council for Long Beach Staff, Tasha Hunter, Board President, Lisa DeSmidt, Marketing and Grants Manager, and Griselda Suarez Executive Director; Inlandia Institute and Cati Porter, Executive Director; Los Angeles Poetry Festival and Suzanne Lummis, Director; Avenue 50 Studio Arts Organization and their literary programs La Bloga and Olga García Echeverría and Michael Sedano; Marsha De La O, Phil Taggart, and Gwendolyn Alley for inviting me to present in Ventura and Oxnard; Beyond Baroque Literary Arts Center; Anansi Writers Workshop, The World Stage; Arroyo Arts Collective Poetry in the Windows Awards; and Inner City Cultural Center Talent Fest, 1994

To Mis Amig@s in the Arts, many who've been around for years, for cheering me on, inspiring me, enlightening me, challenging me, and brightening my life with the honor of your friendship:

Rosalind Bell, Veronica Ortega, Mary Torregrossa, Leslie Larson, Carla Trujillo, Suzanne Lummis, Renee Swindle, Frankie Hernandez, Consuelo Flores, Olga García Echeverría, Ruth Nolan, Ralph Carter, Jerry Garcia, Linda Parnell, Berta IJ Graaff, Jessica Ceballos y Campbell, Karineh Mahdessian, Rashaan Alexis Meneses, Irene Suico Soriano, Marisela Norte, and Womxn's Write Inn: Lisbeth Coiman, Risa Vinzant, Deb Jensen, Sehba Sarwar, Alicia Vogl Saenz, Marta Mora, Tisha Reichle, and Lucy Rodriguez-Hanley

To My Family for sticking together: Mama, Gary Avance, and my magnificent sisters Cynthia Duran, Michelle La Fontaine, Monique La Fontaine-Tomaso, and Quinta Avance, their spouses, and children

To Chacho Rory Martin González for keeping me company, entertaining me, and forcing me to get up and move when I work on my writing endeavors and Uptown Word & Arts programming

And to Jorge Martin for your love, driver services, never failing support, quick and insightful wit, and for sharing your life-journey with me. You've put almost as much work into this book as I have

About the Author

liz gonzález, a fourth generation Southern Californian, grew up near Route 66 in the San Bernardino Valley. Her poetry, fiction, and creative nonfiction have been published widely. Her work has appeared in *Inlandia: A Literary Journey*, *Border Senses Literary Magazine*, the *San Francisco Chronicle*, among other journals and periodicals, and in the anthologies *Voices from Leimert Park Anthology Redux*, *The Coiled Serpent: Poets Arising from the Cultural Quakes and Shifts of Los Angeles*, *Wide Awake: The Poets of Los Angeles and Beyond*, among others. She is the author of *Beneath Bone* (Manifest Press, 2000), a limited edition collection of poems. *Dancing in the Santa Ana Winds: Poems y Cuentos New and Selected* is her first full-length book.

Her awards include a 2017 Residency at Kimmel Harding Nelson Center for the Arts, a 2016 Incite / Insight Award from the Arts Council for Long Beach, a 2014 Irvine Fellowship at the Lucas Artists Residency Program at the Montalvo Arts Center, Arroyo Art Collective's Poetry in the Windows awards, a Macondo Foundation Casa Azul Writers Residency, a residency at Hedgebrook: A Retreat for Women Writers, an Arts Council for Long Beach Professional Artist Fellowship, and a fiction writers grant from The Elizabeth George Foundation.

She co-founded and directs Uptown Word & Arts, promoting literacy and the arts, is a proud member of Macondo Writers Workshop, serves on the Macondo 2018 Ad Hoc Advisory Board, and is a creative writing instructor for the UCLA Extension Writers' Program.

lizgonzalez.com

ABOUT
LOS NIETOS PRESS

Los Nietos Press is dedicated to the countless generations of people whose lives and labor created the world community that today spreads over the coastal floodplain known simply as Los Angeles.

We take our name from the Los Nietos Spanish land grant that was south and east of the downtown area. Our purpose is to serve local writers so they may share their words with many, in the form of tangible books that can be held and read and passed on. This written art form is one way we realize our common bonds and help each other discover what is meaningful in life.

LOS NIETOS PRESS
www.LosNietosPress.com
LosNietosPress@Gmail.com

Made in the USA
San Bernardino, CA
03 July 2018